Paula Fox

The Library of Author Biographies™

Paula Fox

Susanna Daniel

rosen
central™

The Rosen Publishing Group, Inc., New York

For John

Published in 2004 by The Rosen Publishing Group, Inc.
29 East 21st Street, New York, NY 10010

Library of Congress Cataloging-in-Publication Data

Daniel, Susanna.
Paula Fox / by Susanna Daniel.— 1st ed.
   p. cm. — (The library of author biographies)
Summary: Discusses the life and work of this popular author, including her writing process and methods, inspirations, a critical discussion of her books, biographical timeline, and awards.
Includes bibliographical references and index.
ISBN 0-8239-4525-1 (library binding)
1. Fox, Paula—Juvenile literature. 2. Authors, American—20th century—Biography—Juvenile literature. 3. Children's stories—Authorship—Juvenile literature. [1. Fox, Paula. 2. Authors, American. 3. Women—Biography. 4. Authorship.]
I. Title. II. Series.
PS3556.O94Z73 2004
813'.54—dc21

                                                    2003009176

Manufactured in the United States of America

Table of Contents

Introduction:
Room to Grow

At eighty years of age, Paula Fox is considered one of the most out-standing and talented writers for children living today. Critics and reviewers have time and again praised her honest, straightforward development of intense, complex, and often tragic stories, as well as her captivating use of language. Fox's characters are often in crisis, confronting serious challenges such as homelessness, illness in the family, or a parent's death. Rather than shrink in the face of hardship, Fox's characters use their imaginations and courage to triumph, often without the assistance of adults.

To date, Paula Fox has written twenty-three books for children, including *The Slave Dancer* (1973), which won the American Library Association's distinguished Newbery Medal in 1974, and *The Little Swineherd and Other Tales* (1978), which was nominated for the National Book Award in 1979. Fox's body of work for young people was awarded the prestigious Hans Christian Andersen Award in 1978. Fox has also written six novels for adults and a memoir, or autobiography, entitled *Borrowed Finery* (1999), which was a finalist for the National Book Critics Circle Award in 2000.

Fox's characters often deal with rather intense situations in their lives, and many of Fox's novels have been called "somber," "dark," and "emotional." They've also been called "honest," because in her books, as in real life, there are no easy answers, and there isn't always a hero or heroine who saves the day. Fox's protagonists rely on their own resources—their intelligence and determination—to find their way in the world. Ultimately, at the heart of each of her books is a difficult journey of one kind or another—a journey made not only by Fox's characters, but also by her readers.

For example, take Paul Coleman, the adolescent protagonist of *Radiance Descending* (1997), whose younger brother, Jacob, has Down's syndrome. Jacob requires a lot of their parents' attention, and Paul often feels neglected. When the Colemans move from Long Island to New York City, Paul decides to start avoiding his younger brother, who has irritating habits like laughing all the time and messing up Paul's room. As it turns out, ignoring Jacob takes as much energy as paying attention to him, so Paul tries to find some middle ground. He begins to escort Jacob to his Saturday allergy shots, and through this routine, Paul is introduced to a whole new world—his brother's world. Paul grows to appreciate the slower pace of Jacob's life, and he eventually learns to be more compassionate.

Many of the characters in Fox's books learn the important skill of seeing the world through other people's eyes without being judgmental. After they endure hardships, they have a better understanding of what it is like to be in other people's shoes. Readers, too, gain a sense of compassion after reading about situations that might have previously been unfamiliar to them.

For example, in *Monkey Island* (1991), an eleven-year-old boy named Clay Garrity is abandoned by his father, who has just lost his job. Clay's mother is eight months pregnant and jobless, and she, too, ends up abandoning him in a welfare hotel where they have moved. Clay fears that he will be taken into custody by a social welfare agency, so he runs away to live on the streets. Eventually, he makes friends with two men who have also become homeless due to bad luck, and then he catches a terrible case of pneumonia. By the end of the novel, Clay is reunited with his mother. His experiences on the streets have shown him how difficult life can be, and through this realization, he is able to forgive his mother for abandoning him.

In this novel, like *Radiance Descending* and many others, Fox explores the themes of alienation and abandonment, resilience and resourcefulness, and compassion. Readers of *Monkey Island* who are not familiar with homelessness can learn through Clay's experiences how lonely and scary living on the streets can be. Readers will also come to realize that what happened to Clay's family could possibly happen to anyone.

In order to get across such somber and emotional stories, Fox chooses to write in a simple, clear, and direct writing style, with lots of suspense driving the story. Fox uses some advanced vocabulary words and writes about confusing emotional situations because she doesn't believe in talking down to young people or sugarcoating misfortune in order to protect them. Readers looking for laugh-out-loud stories that will have them in stitches from the first page to the last won't find that in Paula Fox's novels. Instead, they will find true-to-life characters with imagination, intelligence, and resilience. They will also find an author who respects children and adolescents as much as adults and who knows that they have lessons to teach as well as to learn.

1 A Fragmented Childhood

Paula Fox was born in New York City on April 22, 1923. Her childhood was not an easy one. Her mother, Elsie, was a hardhearted woman and a reluctant mother, and her father, Paul, was an on-again, off-again screenwriter and novelist. When Paula was only a few days old, Elsie and Paul left her in an orphanage; her grandmother, Candeleria, who traveled too much to care full-time for a child, placed Paula in the care of a kind couple who already had several children.

The family had too much on their hands, however, and soon after, Paula was given to a local minister named Reverend Elwood Amos

Corning. The reverend lived in Balmville, New York. For most of the first eight years of her life, Paula lived with Reverend Corning—whom she knew as Uncle Elwood—in an old Victorian house. They lived with the reverend's mother, who was kind but rarely spoke. Meanwhile, Paula's father kept irregular contact with Reverend Corning, sent money from time to time, and appeared one afternoon when Paula was five years old, only to leave again the next day.

Brief visits with her parents would become normal in Paula's life; when her parents returned, it was never for long. Shortly after Paul's visit, when she was five, Paula's parents sent for her to join them in Hollywood, California. Paula was there for only a few days before her mother, Elsie, decided she'd had enough—she wasn't cut out for motherhood, she said—and Paula was sent away again, this time to live with a friend named Mrs. Cummings, in Redlands, California.

From Redlands, Paula visited her parents four or five times. The attention she received from them was unpredictable and sometimes frightening. Her father, who was an alcoholic, frequently referred to her as "Pal" and her mother was distant, cold, and sometimes cruel.

After a year with Mrs. Cummings, Uncle Elwood showed up in California to take Paula back to the East Coast. Paula was grateful and relieved, but the blessing was short-lived. Paula had lived only a few short weeks with Uncle Elwood before her mother's mother, Candeleria, arrived to take Paula into her custody. Having to move in with her grandmother at age eight was a terrible disappointment for Paula. In her memoir, she wrote, "My parting from the minister was an amputation."[1]

An Early Love of Reading

Despite the turbulence of her early years, it was during this time that Paula began to realize that books were dependable friends. She remembers Uncle Elwood reading aloud to her from classic children's stories such as *Robin Hood*, *King Arthur and the Knights of the Round Table*, *Treasure Island*, and *Aesop's Fables*, among others. When she was only five years old, Paula learned her first lesson in how ideas translate into stories or words. She was sitting with Uncle Elwood as he prepared his sermon for the following Sunday. Uncle Elwood was stumped and asked the little girl for suggestions. She had been thinking about a recent picnic, where they had sat so close to the spray of a cascade that the water dampened their sandwiches. She told him he should write about waterfalls.

That Sunday, as she sat in the congregation at Sunday services, she was startled to realize that Uncle Elwood had taken her advice—the sermon was, indeed, about a waterfall. Even at her young age, Paula began to understand that words were meaningful and could inspire emotion, thought, and imagination. This was her first inspiration to become a writer.

These events, and the support of Uncle Elwood, encouraged young Paula to become an avid reader. In an essay Fox later wrote about the importance of books in her childhood, she said:

> I was taught to read when I was five. The old house where I lived in those days [with Uncle Elwood] was filled with books and not much else. The roof leaked, the well was always going dry, the wallpaper peeled, the furniture was patched and mended, the driveway up the long hill to the house was impassable in heavy rain or snow, and there was never enough money for repairs.
>
> But the books! They lined the walls of the rooms; they stood in columns on the floor; they were piled up in the attic on top of a river of

National Geographic [magazines] that cascaded down the crowded attic stairs.

In bad weather, when I couldn't go outside, I used to sit on those stairs and extract a *Geographic* as carefully as if I were playing pick-up sticks, so I wouldn't bring the whole attic down on myself. Among the glossy pages of the magazines, I met up with pygmies and Balinese dancers, cities built on water, mountain peaks yet unscaled, desert people and people who lived amid eternal snow, dragonflies and anacondas. On those attic stairs in an old house that seemed always on the verge of collapse, I began to sense huge possibilities.[2]

A Roller-coaster Adolescence

Paula lived for a while in a small brick house on Long Island with her grandmother and two uncles. She attended Public School 99, a one-room schoolhouse that stood next to a large cemetery. Paula, who was curious and adventuresome even at that young age, visited the cemetery every chance she could. She spent a lot of time by herself, exploring and using her imagination to make up wild fantasies. Paula's classmates on Long Island didn't know what to make of her—she was fair-haired and might have been mistaken for Swedish or Finnish if not for the dark skin and hair of her grandmother. She was teased off and on by her peers. In her memoir, *Borrowed Finery*, Fox explained how living with her grandmother made it difficult for her to fit in:

> One morning my grandmother made me a different breakfast from the usual toast and cereal. She minced garlic and spread it on a slice of bread that had been soaked in olive oil My arrival at school was greeted by my classmates with cries of mock disgust, hands outstretched to keep me at a distance.
>
> I was the foreigner in a school population made up largely of children from working-class Irish Catholic families. The final . . . evidence of my foreignness was my grandmother herself, when she appeared in school on those days set aside for parents to visit classes.
>
> She did not resemble any other mother. She was older, of course. And she had a thick Spanish accent . . . But I loved the bread soaked in oil and covered with garlic, and I didn't give it up once I'd tasted it.[3]

When two other foreigners arrived at the school—a French Canadian boy and an Armenian boy—Fox formed an alliance with them, accepting and even celebrating the ways she was different from most of her classmates. She wrote in her memoir that garlic was her saving grace, confirming her position as an outsider at her school. If not for the garlic, she might have continued trying to fit in and to be like everyone else, though it was clear even this early in her life, with her turbulent background and her love for reading and being alone, that she was different.

Off to Cuba

Soon, Paula left Public School 99 because she and her grandmother moved to Cuba to spend more than a year on a sugar plantation owned by a cousin. She didn't know where Cuba was, exactly, but she found it in an atlas at school. To Paula's eyes, the country looked like a green lizard lying across a blue sea.

On the plantation in Cuba, Paula had plenty of space to roam and play, including acres of manicured gardens on the estate where she and her grandmother lived, but she had few friends or companions. Her grandmother was busy most of the day tending to the cousin who owned the plantation. It was a while before Paula started school and made friends among her classmates and with her teacher, Señora García, who was in charge of one classroom full of children of all ages. In her memoir, Fox recounts vivid memories from this time:

> During my many months in Cuba, my grandmother had taken me to visit Tía Laura, my real great-aunt. She was retired, by then, and living in the country. We had supper with her and afterward went into the wild moonlit garden. A fire burned beneath a large black cauldron. I recall that she wore a black dress, silvered by the moonlight, and stirred *dulce de leche*, a Cuban sweet, with a huge ladle.[4]

While in Cuba, Paula wrote letters to Uncle Elwood. The only time she didn't receive a reply right away was when his mother, the silent but kind woman who had lived with Paula for the first eight years of her life, passed away. Though the woman wasn't Paula's own grandmother, she was sad for Uncle Elwood and remembered the woman fondly.

The Birth of a Storyteller

Though Paula and her grandmother were never very close, the person Paula would become as an adult was greatly determined by her grandmother's passion for storytelling. Candeleria told Paula stories from her life in Spain. These were sometimes funny, sometimes dreadful. As Fox would later recall, "What I [remember] most about her stories, told to me in fragments over the years I lived with her, was an underlying sorrowful tone, a puzzled mourning for the past."[5] Though she'd learned to love reading stories while in Uncle Elwood's care, it was perhaps Paula's grandmother who helped her make the leap from merely reading stories to telling them herself.

In September 1933, a revolution was led by Communist Fulgencio Batista Zalvidar (called Batista) against the liberal government of Gerardo Machado, then the president of Cuba. For several years, Cuba's economy had been deteriorating, and the price for sugar had dropped to all-time lows, despite the United States's support for the Machado government. In the midst of the chaos, facing a new Communist government, Paula and her grandmother fled to Long Island. In comparison to the sugar plantation, the one-room apartment they returned to was very small and crowded. By this time, Paula was ten years old and had already lived in more homes than many people do in a lifetime. She returned to P.S. 99, and immediately it seemed as if she'd never left at all. She began visiting regularly with her uncles and cousins in Spanish Harlem and she and her cousin Natalie often went to the movies.

During this time in New York, Paula continued to cultivate her love of reading. She and a few other schoolgirls found an abandoned shed near her apartment and decided to use it as a library. They collected and shared all of their books and dug up a few pieces of old furniture from the neighborhood. Eventually, winter came, and the shed grew too cold for the girls to continue meeting there. By the time they had to abandon it, however, Paula had acquired a real library card.

Family Reunion

When Paula was eleven, her parents returned to New York from Europe, where they had been living for several years. Paula went to meet their ship where it docked on the Hudson River and watched as Paul and Elsie walked down the gangplank to the pier. As they descended from the ship, in their sunglasses and fine clothes, Paula thought they looked as handsome as movie stars.

However glamorous they seemed, Paula soon learned that her parents had fallen on hard times. During the next month, while she continued to live with her grandmother and visit her parents occasionally, her father gave her a typewriter as a present, then took it back from her to sell it for cash. He also borrowed fifty dollars that Paula had been given by her aunt in Cuba. When, shortly thereafter, he sold a movie script for a large sum, he neither offered to return the typewriter—which naturally Paula had cherished, even for the short time she had it—nor repay the debt. Paula, thinking both debts too small to mention and fearing her parents' anger, kept quiet.

During this period, Paula spent one memorable afternoon shopping for shoes with Elsie, the mother she barely knew, at a department store on Fifth Avenue. The event was arranged by Paul, who every so often encouraged Elsie to spend more time with Paula. As Fox would later recount:

> She bought me two pairs of handsome shoes, one black kidskin, the other green suede. During the time that we were together, it felt as if we were continually being introduced to each other. I was conscious of an immense

strain, as though a large limp animal hung from my neck, its fur impeding my speech.

Each time, each sentence, I had to start anew. I could hear effort in her voice, too. The whole transaction, selecting, fitting, paying, wrapping, took less than twenty-five minutes. She smiled brilliantly at me in the elevator descending; the smile lasted a few seconds too long.

"Can you get home by yourself?" she asked me, as though I had suddenly strayed into the path of her vision. I nodded wordlessly. The shopping spree was over.[6]

Paula and her grandmother moved into a larger apartment along with Paula's uncle, Vincent, who woke everyone from sleep at night with loud nightmares. Once, they spent a long holiday weekend with Paula's parents on Martha's Vineyard. Months later, Paula left the Long Island apartment she shared with her grandmother and traveled with her parents by car to Florida, where they had planned to live together in a house that belonged to a friend of Elsie's. But a few days after they arrived at the house in Florida, Elsie and Paul changed their minds once again and drove back to New York, leaving Paula behind with only the housekeeper to look after her.

Paula felt they had not abandoned her so much as they had simply forgotten she existed altogether. She felt trapped by her age—twelve—because she was far too young to leave Florida and start a life on her own.

Life in Florida

Paula went to public school in East Jacksonville, Florida. She made a few friends, including a boy named Matt, who taught her how to scare away water moccasins (a type of poisonous snake) from the nearby wharf by jumping on the wharf before walking on it, and Mattie, an African American girl who worked in the house where Paula lived and with whom Paula played in the fenced-in yard behind the house. Perhaps her best friend at the time was Lee, a boy a few years older than she, who could already drive. Once, Lee was driving Paula to his house and they came to a stop in front of a huge snake lying across the road, its stomach swollen with a big meal. Fox recalls that Lee got out of the car, lifted the snake with both hands, and carried it to the side of the road. This showed not only courage but also a touching sensitivity toward animals that left quite an impression on Paula.

It was during Paula's time living in Florida that her father announced that he and Elsie were getting a divorce. He arrived in the spring to deliver the news and told Paula while they sat together on a bluff, overlooking a wharf and river. "I had not thought of them as married,"[7] Fox wrote. She didn't even understand how Elsie was enough of a real human being, made of flesh and blood, to have carried Paula in her belly for nine months. To Paula, her mother seemed alien.

After discussing the divorce for a bit, Paula's father abruptly changed the subject to, of all things, smoking cigarettes. At this point in time, Paula was twelve years old. Her father held out a crumpled pack of cigarettes and insisted Paula take one, even after she shook her head. Paula didn't take to smoking right away, but a few weeks later she and her friend Marjorie tried again, and this time the habit stuck. She would continue to smoke into adulthood.

The owner of Paula's house in Florida was a young woman named Mary. She arrived shortly after Paula's father and stayed for a few weeks, treating Paula like a friend and equal. Fox recalls that Mary encouraged her love of reading and books by giving her a copy of the classic novel *The Brothers Karamazov* (1879), by Fyodor Dostoevsky. Paul, who was by this time romantically involved with Mary, drove both Paula and Mary back to New York, and once again, Paula had to say good-bye to the friends she'd made and start her life again—elsewhere.

2 From Chaos into Adulthood

Paula went back to Long Island to her grandmother's apartment and saw her parents only occasionally over the next year or so. By this time, they were both dating other people, and her father's drinking problem was getting worse.

When she was fourteen years old, Paula spent some time with Mary's relatives in West Pittston, Pennsylvania, then drove with Mary to live in a rented house in Peterborough, New Hampshire.

Peterborough was a pretty town and the location of a popular artists' retreat, which lent the place a touch of glamour, as far as Paula was concerned. She was becoming more and more engaged in the world of books, and she was happy to learn that the town where she now lived was once home to Thornton Wilder, the American playwright and novelist, whose work she'd recently read. The estate where he had lived and worked was located deep in the woods, so Paula had to wear snowshoes to reach it. "When I came upon the fieldstone buildings," she wrote, "I forgot my purpose and felt only apprehension. I breathed in the [icy] air. It was still except for the soft slide of snow now and then from tree branches to the ground. I peered through a window into a room already dark in the early fading of daylight."[1]

The time spent in Peterborough was relatively happy for Paula. She was given her own room in Mary's rented home, which overlooked a wide stream. This period was the first time in Paula's life when she spent more than a few days at a time with her father, who was living at the house under the pretense that he was Mary's cousin. (Back then, it would have been considered scandalous for an unmarried woman and man to live in the same house.)

Another highlight of this period in her life was Paula's English class at school. It was here that Paula's teacher introduced her to poetry and Shakespeare. She made several good friends and had a few suitors at the Peterborough school, including a pharmacist's son, who left sodas in her locker as gifts, and a senior who took her to the movies. Mary, who at twenty-five years old was only a decade older than Paula, became her close friend and confidant. It was Mary she would go to with questions about boys and growing up.

But no chapter in Paula's childhood ever lasted very long. Before a year was up in Peterborough, Paula and her father were forced to leave because of his excessive drinking and the rumors about his relationship with Mary. The spring she turned fifteen, Paula lived in a small apartment rented by her father on Manhattan's Upper West Side. Sometimes her father was there, sometimes he wasn't—she never knew exactly where he went or when he would return.

Choosing a Path

When she was about sixteen years old, Paula's father started pressuring her to figure out what she wanted to do with her life. This motivated her to spend several years trying out her various talents and skills. She attended art school, modeled for sculptors, and practiced the piano. She spent several months working and living on Nantucket, an island off the coast of Massachusetts, with a friend and then was notified by her father that she would be attending boarding school in Canada the following year. She returned to Long Island and stayed with her grandmother until it was time to go to school. During this time, she spent one awkward afternoon visiting Elsie, her mother, in the New York apartment Elsie shared with a male companion.

Sainte-Geneviève, the small boarding school Paula attended for a year in Montréal, was housed in a rambling four-story structure. The boarders—the girls who lived on campus—played bridge every night and went to dances and balls with boys from nearby colleges. Paula had little money, so though she was frequently invited to balls or to go on dates, she usually had to borrow nice clothes to wear. She spent the Christmas holiday on Prince Edward Island with her father and Mary—who was, by this time, her stepmother—then later visited with her father in New York City over spring vacation. She had long since realized that in order to see her parents, she had to live apart from them. When they lived together, her parents inevitably fled.

Paula was waiting for her father to pick her up from school when France signed the armistice with Germany in June 1940. She was seventeen at the time. She and her father spent three weeks in a rented house in Halifax, Nova Scotia, then returned to New York City. There, Paul checked Paula into a women-only boarding house and, much to Paula's surprise, enrolled her in the Julliard School. At Julliard, she played piano and took singing lessons, paid for by Mary.

"My life was incoherent to me," Fox wrote about this period in her life. "I felt it quivering, spitting out broken teeth. When I thought of the purposes I had tried to find for myself the last year, to show my father that I 'wanted' something—piano, voice lessons, sculpture, none of the least use to me—when I thought of the madness of my parents where I was concerned, I felt the bleakest misery."[2]

All the time she was searching to find her passion, it was right there under her nose. From the time Uncle Elwood read to her as a little girl through her teen years, Fox had treasured books. It would be many years, however, before she would turn her love for reading into a passion for writing.

Working Life

When she was seventeen, Paula drove to California with a middle-aged woman named

Kay, a friend of Mary's. The trip was arranged by Paula's father. In Los Angeles, Paula's roller-coaster life only got bumpier.

She was briefly married to an actor who was twice her age; she was underage at the time of the wedding, so her father had to give his consent by telegram. The actor left on a merchant ship shortly after Paula found a job as a waitress in a Greek café; he was gone for months, and they broke up after he returned.

Paula stayed in California for eight years after that, working a string of odd jobs. She worked for a magician, then as a painter at a ceramics factory, then as an instructor at Arthur Murray's, a popular dance studio. She made friends with a Hungarian refugee who made designer clothes, and volunteered her services as a model in her friend's fashion shows. For Warner Brothers, a film studio, she read South American novels (using the Spanish skills she learned long ago in Cuba) and wrote reports about their potential as film scripts. It was during this time, when she was twenty years old, that she became pregnant and gave up the baby for adoption because she did not have the means to care for a child. She regretted the decision immediately but could do nothing to reverse it.

The Author Emerges

Fox returned once again to New York in 1948, when she was twenty-five years old. Soon after, she married a man named Richard Sigerson and had two sons, Adam and Gabriel. She divorced Sigerson in 1954 and attended Columbia University from 1955 to 1958, stopping just short of her degree. She taught in various schools in and around New York for the next several years, until 1962, when she married Martin Greenberg, who was a professor of English at C. W. Post College in Greenvale, New York. Martin was also an editor at a literary journal that had rejected Fox's fiction for publication. They are still married today, more than forty years later.

Almost immediately after the wedding, Fox, her sons, and her new husband moved together to Greece to live for six months. Greenberg had won a respected award called a Guggenheim Fellowship, which allowed him to study and work and gave Fox the time and space she needed to begin her career as a novelist. Of this period, Fox recalled:

> I remember when I was finally able to quit my teaching job and devote myself full-time to

writing. People asked me, "But what will you DO?" People have this idea that a life spent writing is essentially a life of leisure. Writing is tremendously hard work. There is nothing more satisfying, but it is work all the same.[3]

In Greece, with the time and support she needed, Fox wrote her first adult novel, *Poor George* (1967), followed shortly by her first children's novel, *Maurice's Room. A Likely Place* and *How Many Miles to Babylon?* (1967) were published soon thereafter. Once she'd committed to writing books, publication followed relatively easily. Though she is more widely known as a writer for young people, her adult novels have gained much critical praise.

Fox has said that she never consciously decided to write for either kids or adults. She believes that first and foremost she tells a story for herself, and the audience comes second. She has been fortunate in that her books for children and young adults have provided her the time and resources to write her less widely known books for adults. She said that she is especially interested in writing about children because they are experiencing many things for the first time, including life's small daily surprises as well as periods of loneliness and challenging events. She also has said that writing for children is not very different from writing for adults, because children also know about the difficult themes she explores in her adult work—for example, pain, betrayal, fear, and unhappiness—and they don't need be protected from these harsh realities.

3 The Pleasure of Telling Stories

Fox's love for reading and storytelling was awakened and nurtured by her earliest father figure, Uncle Elwood, who read to her from a young age, and was encouraged by her grandmother, Candeleria, who told Fox zany stories about her life in Spain. Because of her experiences, Fox believes in teaching children to appreciate books from early in life, as soon as they can read. "Imagination can be . . . stifled," she says, "[b]ut it can be awakened. When you read to a child, when you put a book in a child's hands, you are bringing that child news of the . . . nature of life. You are an awakener."[1]

Fox believes that having a fertile imagination is the key to good storytelling. For her, storytelling depends more on imagination than on capturing real-life experiences. Sometimes, however, she uses her memories as a starting point for her novels, and like a tadpole turning into a bullfrog, the stories grow in an entirely new direction and take on lives of their own.

For example, one part of the book *One-Eyed Cat* (1984) was influenced by an experience Fox had when she was a child. In *One-Eyed Cat*, the main character, Ned, accidentally wounds a stray cat with an air rifle (a gun that shoots pellets or BBs using compressed air) and is tormented by guilt as a result—even to the point of becoming physically ill. He has kept his shameful secret to himself, and he believes that his shame will get bigger and bigger, haunting him for the rest of his life.

Although this story never happened to Fox as it is told, it was inspired by a memory from Fox's childhood, which she recalls in her memoir:

> Once the [neighbor] children brought along a sickly puppy and showed it to me. We passed its limp body among us, caressed it, and at last killed it with love. We stared,

stricken, at the tiny dog lying dead in the older boy's hands, saliva foaming and dripping from its muzzle.

Later that day, after the farmer and his family had departed, I told the minister I had had a hand in the death of the little animal. Although he tried to comfort me, to give me some sort of absolution, I couldn't accept it for many years.

Even now, I am haunted from time to time by the image of a small group of children, myself among them, standing silently at the back door of the house, looking down at the corpse.[2]

Notice how Fox has taken this sad, true-life memory and used her imagination and writing skills to transform it into *One-Eyed Cat*. It is because of her own familiarity with the shame and guilt of wounding a defenseless animal that she is able to write with authority and compassion about Ned's predicament.

Understanding Human Behavior

As previously mentioned, an active imagination can help both the author and the reader understand the circumstances of other people's lives and have more compassion. One important tool in novel writing is psychology, which is the science of the way people behave, especially in challenging situations. Successful authors must be very smart psychologists and always have their characters behave realistically, or else their readers won't believe a word they write. A big difference between psychologists who see patients and writers who develop characters is that the patients are real and the characters are fictional (though they might be loosely based on real memories). A writer can't make up realistic fictional characters, though, without using his or her imagination.

Paula Fox has a thorough understanding of human psychology. She understands human behavior as well as any children's author working today, and her complicated stories and character development prove it.

Take nineteen-year-old Ben, the main character in Fox's novel *Blowfish Live in the Sea* (1970). Ben hasn't spoken to his father in twelve years, and he has the odd habit of constantly writing the sentence "Blowfish live in the sea" on anything and everything in sight. Ben is a strange kid, and you might not understand him if you met him on the street.

Ben developed his quirky habit when he was a child, after his father came back from a trip to the Amazon with a souvenir gift: a painted blowfish. Ben was too smart for his dad, because he knew that blowfish didn't live in rivers—they live in the sea, which meant that his father had lied about where he'd gone. This one lie causes Ben so much pain that he doesn't speak to his father for twelve years.

During the course of the novel, Ben and his sister, Carrie, travel from New York to Boston to visit their father, and along the way begin to understand more about their past and each other. Because she understands human behavior and writes so well, Fox is able to communicate Ben's sad and strange life to the reader, inspiring compassion and tenderness.

Challenges Bring Opportunities

Like her characters, Fox had to undertake a long journey to finally find a place she could call home—she'd lived in New York, Florida, California, Pennsylvania, New Hampshire, Cuba, Canada, and Greece by the time her career as a writer was under way. After that, things started to settle down for her, and years later, in 1971, one of her adult novels, *Desperate Characters* (1970), was made into a film starring legendary actress Shirley MacLaine. With the money from the movie, she and Greenberg bought a century-old townhouse in Brooklyn, New York. Fox said in an interview with the newspaper, the *Hartford Courant*, that she was forty-seven years old when she bought the house in Brooklyn, but this was the first time in her life that she felt she'd found a true home. She and her husband have lived in the townhouse for more than thirty years now. Her two sons from her second marriage are grown men.

Life has not ceased to throw challenges into her path, however, and Fox continues to turn hardship into opportunity. About a decade ago, Fox was contacted by a woman who turned out to be the daughter she had given up for adoption when she was only twenty years old. In her memoir, Fox recalled the Saturday morning when she was sitting in her kitchen and a thick Federal Express envelope arrived. There was a hand-written note on top of a letter, and it said, "Go slow."[3]

Fox knew right away whom the envelope was from and what it contained. She called upstairs to her husband, "She's found me!"[4]

Fox's daughter's name is Linda. The two women exchanged letters for three months, sometimes twice a day. Then they arranged to meet each other in San Francisco, where, they agreed, if they got bored of each other, they would have other things to entertain them. But they didn't get bored of each other. As soon as they met in the airport, they sat down and talked animatedly for two hours. "She was the first woman related to me I could speak to freely,"[5] wrote Fox.

Paula and Linda have remained close, and Paula is also involved in the lives of Linda's children, her grandchildren. In fact, one of her grandchildren is a musician named Courtney Love, the leader of the grunge band Hole and widow of the popular Nirvana lead singer, Kurt Cobain. Fox said in an interview that Courtney reminds her of her own mother, Elsie. "[Linda] also told me that the reason [Courtney's] last name is Love," said Fox in the same interview, "is that Linda used to say, 'Courtney, love, come here.'"[6]

In 1997, Fox had another life-changing experience. While traveling in Israel with her husband, Fox was mugged by a man who struck her, took her purse, and left her bleeding from her head. She spent three weeks in a Jerusalem hospital and one week in Columbia Presbyterian Hospital, in New York City. All in all, it took nearly a year for her to get better. "It took me three months to write the first ten pages of [my memoir, *Borrowed Finery*],"[7] she told a reporter. In another interview, she explained how her discipline got her through her recovery.

> I wrote every morning, because my energy was highest then. I would get up at eight or eight-thirty, and start and play solitaire, and go to the typewriter, and play solitaire, and go to the typewriter. There were days when I couldn't move beyond a sentence, and then other days when I could write a whole page. There were days when I knew what I was about to do, and then I would go with relative speed—it would take me three hours to write two or three paragraphs. So those days encouraged me, for all the bleak times in between.[8]

One positive thing came from the nightmarish ordeal, however: after she recovered from her injury, she found that she no longer cared for cigarettes. This was no small change in her life, since she'd been a regular smoker since that first taste of cigarettes in Florida when she was twelve years old.

4 Realistic Characters and Themes

Overall, Fox's books are less concerned with plot than with character, meaning that what happens is less important than how the characters cope with the events of their lives. Many characters in Fox's novels find themselves in strange situations with no one to rely on but themselves. Many of her characters, too, are coping with the illness or death of a family member and the loneliness and grief that results.

For example, *The Village by the Sea* (1988)—a book for middle school readers—is about a ten-year-old girl named Emma who is sent to live with her unkind, alcoholic aunt for two weeks while her father recovers from surgery in the hospital. Emma copes with her anxiety about her father's health and her cruel aunt by building a miniature "village" on the beach with her new friend, Bertie. But because it is made of sand, the village is destined for destruction. Emma enjoys building the village so much that she isn't bothered much when it is destroyed. Afterward, she cherishes the memory of her creation. She returns home with a new sense of courage and compassion for her aunt. In *The Village by the Sea*, as in life, nothing lasts forever, and one's memories are ultimately as important as one's present-day reality.

Another of Fox's recurring themes appears in *A Likely Place* (1967), the story of a nine-year-old named Lewis who is so exasperated by the intrusion of the adults in his life that he thinks about running away. Adults are constantly taking Lewis places without asking him where he wants to go, telling him what he is feeling, and assigning him activities he doesn't enjoy and isn't good at. This leaves him feeling lonely, alienated, and misunderstood.

When Lewis's parents go away on a business trip and leave him with a fascinating, oddball babysitter named Miss Fitchlow, he gets a taste of what it's like to live without pushy adults around. Miss Fitchlow engages him in intelligent conversations, introduces him to yoga exercise and health foods, and allows him to go to the park alone. During the course of his time with Miss Fitchlow, Lewis carves out a place of his own in the park near his home. It becomes his private place where he can be alone with his thoughts and keep personal items like a candle and a pamphlet he found. He also befriends a man named Mr. Madruga, who doesn't speak English perfectly and needs Lewis to help him translate an important letter to his son.

In the end, Lewis's overprotective but well-meaning parents return, and Lewis greets them with a stronger sense of who he is and where he wants to go in the world. They haven't especially changed, but he has, which is the most important thing. Like many of Fox's books, *A Likely Place* has as much wisdom to teach to parents as it does to children.

Another one of Fox's novels for younger readers, *Dear Prosper* (1968), is narrated by an old dog who is writing a letter to one of his former owners, telling about the events that have occurred in his life. The story begins with the dog's birth behind a general store in New

Mexico, then continues through his escape to another town, where he is adopted and renamed by a sheriff. Prosper goes on to work as a ranch dog, and then to live in the lap of luxury with a rich new owner. He continues on many adventures and ends up living with a kind caretaker; in the end, he has led a contented life. Ultimately, the book is about overcoming hardships and long journeys.

Fox is able to capture a dog's view of his own life and at the same time, she relates the dog's long journey to that of most human beings. Like a human, Prosper forms loyal relationships as well as painful ones, overcomes hardships and adversaries, and at long last arrives at his true home, where he can feel both loved and needed.

Understanding Kids

Time and again, even in her early novels, Fox has proved that she has a great understanding of young people—even peculiar young people, like the main character of her first novel for young adults, *Maurice's Room* (1966). Maurice is an eight-year-old boy who is obsessed with collecting things. Maurice's collections aren't especially valuable or prizewinning; among his rare finds is a bottle full of dead beetles, a raccoon tail, rocks, and anything else that captures his imagination.

Only Maurice and his friend Jacob, who shares his love of collecting, are able to walk around in his junk-filled room without knocking items off their shelves. Maurice's parents are at their wit's end— they consider their son's collections "junk" and encourage him to pursue what they call more "constructive" and less peculiar interests. They force him to take trumpet lessons, which he hates. One day, though, they give Maurice a toy sailboat, which he loves, until he accidentally destroys it midsail when he and Jacob become distracted by some rusty bedsprings they spot in the pond.

When Maurice's parents decide to move to the country, Maurice gives the bedsprings to Jacob but packs up the rest of his collections, all of which are lost when the moving van goes over a bump and the back door opens accidentally. However, Maurice is consoled when he discovers that the barn at his new home is filled with unknown treasures, and he starts to build his collections all over again. During the course of the book, it is Maurice's parents who have to learn the difficult lesson of compassion; by the end, they have come to accept their son's passion for collecting. Many of Fox's young characters end up teaching their parents or other adults important lessons, instead of the other way around.

The Critics Weigh In

Critics have consistently praised Fox's sympathy with and portrayal of children, parents, and their often troubled relationships with each other and with the world at large. Notable children's literature critic Zena Sutherland wrote, "The special gift of Paula Fox is that of seeing from the child's viewpoint and maintaining that viewpoint while feeling the sympathy of an adult and the detachment of an artist. Her children move our hearts because they are so true, yet there is neither sentimentality nor pity in her writing."[1]

Critics also have praised Fox's clear writing style, her honesty, and her willingness to confront complicated and emotional issues. They are especially complimentary of Fox's characterization of adult characters, who are as likely to be as flawed and mixed-up as their kids—if not more so. Another critic wrote in the *New York Times Book Review*, "In an era when youthful distrust of adults is rampant, Miss Fox remains true to the concept that children need adults if they are to grow, though they must be fulfilled themselves and accept young people as individuals."[2]

It hasn't escaped the attention of the reviewers (all of whom are adults, by the way) that Paula Fox's writing style and choice of themes pay respect to her young readers. She does this by challenging readers to confront difficult writing and complicated topics, which is a sign of respect and admiration. Neither has it gone unnoticed that Fox's preference is for dark, emotional, complicated stories. One reviewer wrote in *Literature Resource Center*, "In her best children's books, Fox manages to discover what it is to be a vulnerable child struggling for a sure sense of self in a bewildering and often alien world."[3]

Critic John Rowe Townsend had this to say: "Of the new writers for children who emerged in the United States in the later 1960s, Paula Fox was quickly seen to be one of the most able. Her books were unusually varied; each had a distinct individual character, but at the same time each was stamped with her own imprint."[4]

A Darker Side

Many of Fox's books, especially those for adolescent readers, are darker in theme and tone than *The Village by the Sea* and *A Likely Place*. In these novels, Fox's writing is mysterious, somber, and thoughtful. Her most well-known novel, *The*

Slave Dancer (1973), is a good example of Fox's willingness to challenge young readers with difficult stories full of hardship and issues like slavery and racism. The novel takes place in the 1840s, and it is the story of a thirteen-year-old boy named Jessie, who is kidnapped from his hometown of New Orleans and put on a slave ship bound for West Africa. (Slave ships were sent during the slave trade to capture Africans and bring them back to the United States to work against their will.) Jessie is kidnapped because he plays the fife—a musical instrument that resembles a small flute without keys—and, after the ship reaches America and starts the voyage home again, he is forced to play music to the captured slaves so they will dance and exercise their limbs, which become cramped from living in too small a space during the journey across the Atlantic Ocean.

During the course of his journey back from Africa, Jessie befriends a slave boy named Ras, who is about his age. Eventually, Jessie and Ras escape the ship when the crew and many of the slaves drown in a storm. After a terrible struggle, they reach shore safely and are forced to go their separate ways although they have grown as close as brothers. Ras flees to the north, where he can be free, and Jessie makes his way back down south to New Orleans. Changed forever, Jessie finds that not only is he alienated from the home he once knew, but he also cannot stand the sound of music.

In addition to being a good example of Fox's more serious themes, *The Slave Dancer* is also written in Fox's straightforward and gripping style. The opening paragraphs indicate the somber tone of the book:

> In a hinged wooden box upon the top of which was carved a winged fish, my mother kept the tools of her trade. Sometimes I touched a sewing needle with my finger and reflected how such a small object, so nearly weightless, could keep our little family from the poor house and provide us with enough food to sustain life—although there were times when we were barely sustained.
>
> Our one room was on the first floor of a brick and timber house which must have seen better times. Even on sunny days I could press my hand against the wall and force the moisture which had coated it to run to the floor in streams. The damp sometimes set my sister, Betty, to coughing which filled the room with barking noises like those made by quarrelling animals. Then my mother would mention how fortunate we were to live in

A Note of Controversy

In 1974, *The Slave Dancer* won the Newbery Medal, and one critic called the book Fox's "most substantial work . . . a historical novel of weight and intensity which stands on its own, at a distance from her other books."[5] Another critic wrote that the novel "is historical fiction at its finest, for Fox has meticulously researched every facet of the slave trade and of the period."[6] Many critics agree that the novel is so sophisticated that it verges on being a book for adults rather than adolescents.

Some critics, however, had concerns about how the slaves were depicted in the book, as depressed or passive, and accused Jessie of never taking a stand against slavery despite his friendship with Ras, the slave boy.

Most reviewers, though, saw *The Slave Dancer* as a compassionate and fair portrayal of a horrible event. One critic called the novel a "story that movingly and realistically presents one of the most gruesome chapters of history, with all its violence, inhuman conditions, and bestial aspects of human nature—exposed but never exploited."[7]

New Orleans where we did not suffer the cruel extremes of temperature that prevailed in the north.[8]

Even when she is not writing about historical events like the slave trade, Fox's language is never overly dramatic or gimmicky. She always writes with a strong, authoritative style that hooks the reader and maintains interest.

For example, the opening to the previously mentioned *One-Eyed Cat* (the story of the boy who accidentally wounds a cat with an air rifle) is written simply and directly, with no flashy language to confuse the reader. This novel is similar to *The Slave Dancer* in tone and deals with the difficult themes of loneliness and compassion.

Notice how Fox starts from the first paragraph to tell the character's story and reveal his personality to the reader.

Ned Wallis was the minister's only child. The Congregational Church where the Reverend James Wallis preached stood on a low hill above a country lane a mile beyond the village of Tyler, New York. Close by the parsonage, a hundred or so yards from the church, was a small cemetery of weathered tombstones. Some had fallen over and moss and ivy covered them. When Ned first learned to walk, the cemetery was his favorite place to practice. There, his father would come to get him after the members of the congregation had gone home to their Sunday dinners. There, too, his mother often sat on a tumbled stone and watched over him while his father stood at the great church door speaking to each and every person who had attended service that day. That was long ago, before his mother had become ill.[9]

Building Suspense

In the excerpt above, Fox ended the paragraph with a sentence that leaves the reader wanting to know more about Ned's mother and about what will happen to Ned. This narrative tension fuels the reader's desire to continue reading, to know what happens next, and is present in all of Fox's novels. Tension is part of what makes Fox's novels so enjoyable to read.

In *Monkey Island*, the story of the boy who ends up homeless after both his parents abandon him, Fox once again explores themes of alienation, betrayal, and resourcefulness.

The opening of the novel provides a good example of how Fox grips the reader's attention from the first sentence without being overly dramatic with her language.

> Clay Garrity's mother, Angela, had been gone five days from the room in the hotel where they had been living since the middle of October.
>
> On the first evening of her disappearance, he'd waited until long past dark before going to a small table that held a hot plate, a few pieces of china, two glasses and some cutlery as well as their food supply: a jar of peanut butter, half a loaf of bread in a plastic sack, some bananas, a can of vegetable soup, and a box of doughnuts. His mother usually heated soup for their supper and made hot cereal for his breakfast in the pot that sat on the hot plate. Clay lifted the lid. There was nothing inside. During their first week in the hotel, she had made a stew that lasted them for three days. That was the only time she had really cooked.
>
> He ate a banana, then picked up the box of doughnuts. Beneath it, he found twenty-eight dollars and three quarters.
>
> He wasn't especially worried yet about her not coming home. She'd been gone entire days before, not returning until nightfall. But the sight of the money made him uneasy.[10]

Again, Fox uses narrative tension to build suspense and hook the reader from the first page. Why does the money make Clay uneasy? Where has his mother gone? You can be certain that Clay will be faced with difficult challenges throughout the book and likely learn important lessons from his journey—but to know more, you'll have to read it for yourself.

Sophisticated Themes for Sophisticated Readers

Fox's novels for adolescents are not always happy stories. Some of them, in addition to having dark themes, truthfully depict sadness, fear, anger, and desperation, none of which are easy to read about. But readers can always count on Fox to tell an engaging, honest story with a satisfying and realistic conclusion.

A good example of Fox's use of clear language to describe complicated, intense dramatic situations is *How Many Miles to Babylon?* (1967). It is the story of a young black child named James Douglas, who lives with his three aunts in the inner city. James has the habit of telling himself fantastical stories to cope with the harsh realities of his life, including abandonment by his father. Unfortunately, James falls in with a trio of kids who steal dogs and then claim the reward money when it is offered. They are all—including James—forced to go into hiding on Coney Island (in New York) when the police catch on to their scheme.

While in Coney Island, James sees the Atlantic Ocean for the first time and thinks about his roots across the ocean in Africa and about his mother, who is depressed and doesn't live with him. When James leaves the gang and makes it back to the small apartment where he lives, he must decide whether or not to tell the truth about where he's been and what he's been doing. He must also learn to accept the circumstances of his life, including his ill mother and stifling apartment, rather than continue to make up tall tales to escape his troubles.

Critics have said that *How Many Miles to Babylon?* is descriptive, beautifully written, complex, and poetic. "Even though the story is incredibly dark," wrote one reviewer in *Literature Resource Center*, "Fox nevertheless holds out hope for those who, like James . . . can through their own resourcefulness and courage endure in the [hardest] circumstances."[11]

"Resourcefulness" is a word that comes up a lot when referring to Fox's young characters. Like Fox herself when she was a child, her characters are often left alone in difficult or unfamiliar situations, and it is up to them to either find their way back home or create new homes for themselves. The lessons Fox's characters learn in their journeys through childhood are the same ones she learned in hers—to use your imagination to overcome life's difficulties.

In Fox's world—real and fictional—adults aren't always going to be the strong and dependable ones. Sometimes, it is up to the kids—like Emma on the beach in *A Village by the Sea*, Lewis in the park in *A Likely Place*, and Jessie on the slave ship in *The Slave Dancer*—to find their ways without interference or assistance from adults.

Grief and Resilience

In *Monkey Island*, Ned learned how to survive without a home or parents, and he eventually copes with his situation using his own determination and intelligence. Similarly, the thirteen-year-old narrator of *A Place Apart* (1980), Victoria, has to cope with a turbulent home situation when her father unexpectedly passes away. She and her mother are forced to move to a shabby house in another town, and one of Victoria's only new friends is an arrogant boy named Hugh, who tries to manipulate, or bully, her. Within a few months, another obstacle is thrown in her path when her mother announces her plans to remarry.

Eventually, Victoria learns how to manage her grief over her father's death, accept her new home, and form friendships with people who are positive influences. She even comes to accept her mother's new husband.

A reviewer wrote the following about *A Place Apart*:

> Victoria's biggest problem, and one that most adolescents will understand, [is] locating her territory, naming it, making sense of what's happening around her. She used to believe, she tells us, that "If I could describe one entire day of my life to someone, that person would be able to tell me what on earth life was all about." But that was before her father died, and the year that's covered by *A Place Apart* is the period of time it takes her to regain, however shakily, some sense of order and security

. . . *A Place Apart* is a book apart—quiet-voiced, believable, and often very moving.[12]

In many of Fox's books, including *A Place Apart*, characters are thrust into unexpected and challenging situations. Like Paul in *Radiance Descending* (1997) and Ned in *Monkey Island*, Liam, the main character of *Eagle Kite* (1996), must cope with a sudden and dramatic change in his home life when he learns that his father has contracted AIDS and is close to death. This news triggers a memory in Liam from two years earlier, when he saw his father embrace a young man on the beach. Though Liam's mother told him his father contracted the virus through a blood transfusion, Liam suspects otherwise. Meanwhile, his father, who is living apart from Liam and his mother, is wasting away and Liam must come to terms with all his conflicting emotions—anger, denial, shame, forgiveness, and grief. He suspects that his father is gay but cannot come to terms with it, especially since his mother denies it.

Liam's task is not simple, and neither is Fox's portrayal of it. As one critic wrote, "This will be a hard novel for teens to absorb, but well worth the effort."[13]

Times Are Changing

Until the mid-1980s, only a handful of young adult novels about homosexuality existed, and teens looking to read about being gay or having a gay relative were hard-pressed to find quality literature on the subject. The first young adult novel with homosexual content dates back to 1969, when an author named John Donovan wrote a book called *I'll Get There, It Better Be Worth the Trip* about a thirteen-year-old boy named Davy whose new friendship with another boy turns romantic.

For the next fifteen years, books with gay themes were few and far between; in fact, only four young adult novels were published with gay or lesbian themes between the years 1970 and 1976. (They were Isabelle Holland's *The Man Without a Face* [1970], Sandra Scoppetone's *Trying Hard to Hear You* [1974], Rosa Guy's *Ruby* [1976], and Mary W. Sullivan's *What's This About, Pete?* [1976].)

All told, as many as 100 books with gay or lesbian themes have been published for young adults since 1969, Fox's *Eagle Kite* included. Some of these have become instant classics, including Nancy Garden's *Annie on My Mind* (1982), the story of two high school seniors, both girls, who fall in love, and are then torn apart by prejudice. Other popular novels involve main characters who are not gay themselves but who must adjust to having close family members who are gay. *The Arizona Kid* (1986), by Ron Koertge, is the story of a sixteen-year-old boy named Billy who spends the summer in Tucson, Arizona, with his uncle, Wes, an openly gay man with many friends who are HIV-positive. *Jack* (1989), by A. M. Homes, is the story of a boy whose life is disrupted when his father comes "out of the closet."

At one time or another, almost all young adult novels that involve gay or lesbian characters have been challenged by groups who believe the books "promote" homosexuality. A challenge is when a group of parents, community members, or church officials attempts to remove or restrict a book from a school curriculum or library; a ban is the removal of the challenged book. Most challenged books are never removed because concerned parents, teachers, librarians, and other citizens fight to keep the books on library shelves. According to the American Library Association (ALA), which maintains an Office for Intellectual Freedom to keep records of all challenged books, 6,364 books were challenged between 1990 and

2000; of those, 515 were challenged because of material with a homosexual theme. (Other reasons cited for challenging books include sexually explicit material, occult or satanic themes, violence, and offensive language.) *Annie on My Mind*, *The Arizona Kid*, and *Jack* are all listed on the ALA's list of the 100 Most Frequently Banned or Challenged Books.

Despite the fact that challenges to books continue, society has come a long way since 1969—there are now dozens of young adult novels involving gay or lesbian characters on library and bookstore shelves, including Fox's well-loved novel *Eagle Kite*. Many of these contemporary books offer positive and affirming images of gays and lesbians and confront a range of relevant issues, including homophobia, coming out, and acceptance from friends, teachers, parents, and the community.

For Advanced Readers

Fox will never underestimate her readers' ability to understand complicated human dilemmas, and she won't ever write dishonestly about what growing up is like. She doesn't often write funny stories, though a sense of humor can be found throughout her work, especially in *The Little Swineherd and Other Tales*, a collection of short stories modeled after Hans Christian Andersen's folktales in which animal characters are used to satirize, or poke fun at, the way people behave in real life. In most of her novels, Fox uses humor to strengthen her characters' personalities and to enrich, or deepen, their experiences, but the stories themselves are not particularly comic. It might be difficult for some young people to read novels about homelessness, poverty, AIDS, death, and grief, but Fox always delivers a great story and portrays these hardships with honesty and kindness.

5 Recipe for Success

Some people think that writers rely on inspiration to get their work done, but this usually isn't the case. Most writers spend much more time thinking and trying to write than they do actually writing, and Fox is no exception. In an autobiographical essay for Random House, she wrote about the role of discipline in a writer's work.

> As I sit at my typewriter, working, there are moments when I feel I cannot write another word, when the sheer difficulty of discovering what I mean to say and how to say it is so [scary] that I want to stop forever. I haven't yet stopped. I stay in my chair, pen in hand, yellow-lined pad on the desk next

to the machine, doodling or writing down fragments of sentences, hoping some unifying principle will, like a net, draw them together. On the whole, most writing is the questions one asks oneself. What has happened to me? Does it have meaning? It's a peculiar process.[1]

Discovering the meaning of one's experiences is only one part of the puzzle of writing a novel. There's also imagination, psychology, and memory. Each writer's stories depend on his or her observations of human behavior and the world at large, and each writer's perspective, or outlook, is unique. Fox says that everyone's story matters and that each story is one piece of a larger puzzle. The more stories we read, the more we learn about who we are, why we exist, and what kind of world we live in.

Writing a novel also requires the discipline to sit oneself down at a desk or computer even if no words come. It takes discipline to figure out what you want to say and how to say it.

Where Ideas Come From

There's no hard and fast way to make sure you have plenty of things to write about. Some authors say that you should write about what you cannot get off your mind; some say you should write about things that have happened to you or your family. It's not always necessary for a writer to know exactly what she wants to say before sitting down at the computer or typewriter. Sometimes, the story reveals itself after several pages have been written. At this point the author might think to herself, "Aha! So *that's* what I wanted to write about." She might realize that while she thought she wanted to write a story about a girl who lost her cat, she really wanted to write about how the cat had protected her from feeling lonely after the death of a parent. Many writers complete several drafts, or versions, of a story before it is published, which gives them time to discover all the hidden meanings behind their stories. Sometimes what an author intends to write is very different from the final draft. In this way, writing is a very mysterious process.

No matter what an author chooses to write about, the most important aspect of good storytelling is that it reveals something honest about the world and what it means to be human. As Fox wrote in an essay, "Literature is the [territory] of imagination, and stories, in whatever [form], are meditations on life.

[Imagination] is the guardian spirit that we sense in great stories; we feel its rustling."[2]

Metaphors for Life

Fox believes that, in a sense, all stories are metaphors—something that represents something else—for larger stories. For example, in *How Many Miles to Babylon?*, the fantasy stories James tells himself represent his ideal life, free of troubles. (In the novel, James finds a ruby ring on the street and imagines that he is an African prince and the ring is a sign from his mother, who is in Africa preparing a place for him.) And in *One-Eyed Cat*, Ned's refusal to tell his parents about his crime against the cat represents his lack of understanding of human nature and his fear of being judged. When he reveals his secret, his mother teaches him that adults make mistakes, too.

Stories help readers understand the world better without having to go through all the hardships the characters go through. It can be difficult to really understand other people—friends, parents, or strangers—unless we know a great deal about their lives, thoughts, and hopes. Even with all this information, we might think we would behave differently if we were in their shoes. But when an author writes a story about a character—especially if the author writes well and understands human behavior, like Paula Fox—the reader can reach so far inside the mind of the character that he or she can understand the character's behavior. For example, after reading all about the particular circumstance of James's life in *How Many Miles to Babylon?*, it's possible to understand why he joins a dog-napping gang, even if you think dog-napping is morally wrong.

Storytellers like Paula Fox take a given situation—be it sad, challenging, hopeless, or strange—and create a whole world around it, a complicated and realistic human life. It is this ability to inspire compassion that keeps readers coming back to Fox's books decade after decade.

Interview with Paula Fox

SUSANNA DANIEL: You've said that you were unable to write full-time until you and your husband moved to Greece to live. What prompted your desire to be an author, and how long had it been your goal?

PAULA FOX: The six months we rented a house on a Greek island was the first block of time I'd had since I was sixteen. I began a novel, *Poor George*, and completed my first children's book there, *Maurice's Room*. I had written in my early twenties, but my stories were rejected.

SUSANNA DANIEL: If you had to credit two or three people in your life with encouraging you to be a writer, who would they be and how did they influence you?

PAULA FOX: I don't think any familial people encouraged me, although my father, when I saw him, always had books or suggested titles to me. Also, he was a writer, and that may have been one of the elements that led me to writing. My husband, Martin Greenberg, has encouraged me for the last forty years, though, and that has made up for a great deal.

SUSANNA DANIEL: What role do personal experiences and memories play in your fiction? In other words, to what extent has your work been influenced by your life?

PAULA FOX: I wonder if even science fiction isn't, ultimately, about one's personal life or some aspect of one's wishes, also a part of personal life. My life is, after all, the only one I really know deeply; nearly all of my stories arise from it.

SUSANNA DANIEL: You have been writing children's books since the 1960s. How do you think children's literature has evolved since then? Specifically, how have your books, themes, and characters changed?

PAULA FOX: I do believe the significance of children's literature has changed; it's seen as more significant now in the USA. It has always been of significance in England and in Europe in general.

SUSANNA DANIEL: Is there any advice—about life, writing, or anything else—you would give your twelve-year-old self if you could talk to her today?

PAULA FOX: I can't think what advice I would give my twelve-year-old self! Except to wait and see what happens next!

SUSANNA DANIEL: What advice do you have for children who want to be writers when they grow up?

PAULA FOX: I would advise children who wish to be writers to write about their own real experiences and thoughts and feelings as best as they can in whatever form—fairy tale or wizardry or, as it's called, real life—they choose.

SUSANNA DANIEL: You've held an array of jobs in your lifetime. How do you think writing books compares to other careers in terms of happiness and stability?

PAULA FOX: I've had a good many jobs. I always wanted to be a writer but sometimes I wish I weren't! Especially when I'm stuck and must call upon patience with myself to wait out whatever is preventing me from going on with a story.

SUSANNA DANIEL: You've said that discipline helped you write your memoir when you were recovering from your attack in Israel. In your opinion, how important is discipline—as opposed to, say, inspiration or passion—to a writer?

PAULA FOX: From discipline arise passions and inspiration. I go to my study every morning and I start to work. The moments of inspiration are few and far between, but they're worth all the disciplined work that is a preparation for them to arrive.

SUSANNA DANIEL: You seem, from reading your memoir and interviews, to possess an exceptional memory. How important is memory in the writing of fiction?

PAULA FOX: Memory is everything for a writer, especially, in my own case, visual memory.

SUSANNA DANIEL: Writing is a solitary exercise, and many of your books revolve around themes of abandonment, isolation, and alienation. How important is human connection in a writer's life?

PAULA FOX: Human connection to husband, children, friends is everything to some writers, me among them.

SUSANNA DANIEL: Is it essential, in your opinion, for a writer of children's books to have a family? How did your experiences as a mother influence your writing?

PAULA FOX: My experience as a mother did affect my experience as a writer. I saw how a story can be no larger than a mustard seed and yet hold a child's interest. Of course, it must be a very interesting mustard seed!

SUSANNA DANIEL: Do your characters share any of your personal traits? Which ones?

PAULA FOX: My characters share my own traits, especially those I find in other people. If one writes truthfully about oneself, one is usually writing about all the people one has known and that the self contains.

Timeline

1923 Paula Fox is born in New York City on April 22.

1931 Paula is permanently removed from the home where she has been living with a kind minister, Uncle Elwood, and taken, after a few stops, to Cuba to live with her grandmother on a sugar plantation.

1933 Paula and her grandmother return to New York City after a revolution in Cuba. In the next ten years, she lives in New York City, Los Angeles, New Hampshire, and Canada, where she attends boarding school.

1943 Fox gives up a daughter for adoption, then immediately regrets it.

1948 Paula Fox marries Richard Sigerson and has two sons, Adam and Gabriel, shortly after.
1954 Paula and Richard divorce.
1955 Fox enrolls in Columbia University and is a student for three years.
1962 Paula Fox marries Martin Greenberg, an editor whose journal has recently rejected her writing for publication. They move to Greece to live for six months.
1966 Fox publishes her first novel for children, *Maurice's Room*, to positive reviews. Her next two novels, *A Likely Place* and *How Many Miles to Babylon?*, are published within the next year and a half.
1971 Fox's highly praised novel for adults, *Desperate Characters*, is made into a movie starring Shirley MacLaine.
1975 Fox's best-loved and most controversial novel, *The Slave Dancer*, wins the American Library Association's most distinguished prize, the Newbery Medal.
1978 Fox's body of work is awarded the Hans Christian Andersen Award.
1979 *The Little Swineherd and Other Tales* is nominated for the National Book Award.

1983 *A Place Apart* is given the American Book Award.

1990 Around this time, Fox is contacted by the daughter she gave up for adoption forty-seven years earlier. They write to each other, then meet and become friends. They have remained close.

1999 Fox's memoirs, entitled *Borrowed Finery*, are published to rave reviews; the book is a finalist for the National Book Critics Circle Award the following year.

Selected Reviews from *School Library Journal*

Amzat and His Brothers: Three Italian Folktales
1993

Fox retells three Italian folktales that were told to her by a friend who heard them from his grandfather when he was a child growing up in a pre-World War II Italian village. The tales are variations of familiar stories: "Mezgalten," for example, contains elements of "The Brementown Musicians" and "The Wolf and the Kids." Acts of violence may disturb some adults, as in the title story when Amzat and his wife trick his brothers into murdering their wives and then cause the drowning of the brothers. The third story shows the prejudice of villagers toward a woman and her son because of their habit of never bathing and the dull wits of the son. While the woman and son end their days living in a palace (and eventually learning the art of bathing), and the worst of their tormentors end up poorly, the depiction of the heckling is harsh. The people in these stories seem to be more rooted in real life than the usual archetypal folktale characters. A good collection of the region's lore would be welcome, but this isn't the one. McCully's pen-and-ink sketches add little.

The Eagle Kite
1995

Grades 8–12—Liam, a high school freshman, learns that his father is dying of AIDS. Suddenly, his comfortable family is in pieces, and his father has gone to live in a seashore cottage two hours from the family's city apartment. Distanced from both parents by secrets each of them seems compelled to keep, Liam remembers having seen his father embrace a young man years before—a friend, his father had said. In the remainder of the book, Liam and his parents wrestle with truths that encompass not just disappointment and betrayal, but intense love. This is far more than a problem novel. AIDS is integral to the plot, the issue is handled well, and the character who has AIDS is portrayed sympathetically, but the book's scope is broader than that. It is a subtly textured exploration of the emotions of grief that will appeal to the same young people drawn to Mollie Hunter's *A Sound of Chariots* (HarperCollins, 1972) and Cynthia Rylant's *Missing May* (Orchard, 1992). Dramatic tension is palpable, sustained in part by a dazed, timeless quality in Liam's slow reckoning with loss. The characters are neither idealized nor demonized, and Fox's take on Liam as a confused, seethingly angry, tight-lipped, surreptitiously tender teenager has the ring of authenticity. Some in the target audience may find the action too slow or the mood too dark, but those who persevere will be rewarded by the novel's truthfulness

Lily and the Lost Boy
1987
Grades 5–7—Another thought-provoking gem from Fox. Eleven-year-old Lily Corey, her

parents, and her older brother are spending three months on the Greek island of Thasos while Mr. Corey finishes a book. Lily has been flowering—enjoying her friendships with the islanders, her personal study of Greek mythology and archaeology, and her recent closeness with Paul (in their New England home town setting they were "normal" antagonistic siblings). But Lily's summer idyll ends when Paul becomes friendly with another American boy, Jack Hemmings. Jack is mysterious, erratic, defensive, self-destructive, and unloved. Lily resents his influence over Paul and the way in which he disrupts the even, satisfying flow of her lazy summer days. And yet Lily comes closer to an understanding of Jack than anyone, by sharing a catharsis in the young boy's life. Due to Jack's irresponsibility, the Coreys' stay on the island ends with a tragedy that brings the family closer to their unsophisticated Greek friends even as it marks the beginning of a permanent separation. Lily and Paul leave their innocence on Thasos and take away a new awareness of human fragility and dignity. Fox has created a sensitive portrait of three young adolescents who achieve varying degrees of self-knowledge during their stay in an alien but hospitable culture. The story is very low keyed, with lengthy descriptions that capture the atmosphere of the Greek island but that also slow down the pace of the story. Simply written, with strong characterizations and overtones of Greek tragedy, *Lily and the Lost Boy* is an excellent choice for readers who share Lily's own budding characteristics: thoughtfulness, integrity, sensitivity, and courage. A beautifully written story for thoughtful readers.

Monkey Island
1991

Grades 5–7—Eleven-year-old Clay Garrity's family had been what most people would consider an average family—until the magazine his father worked for went out of business and he couldn't find another job over the next year. Clay then experienced the gradual decline from that normal existence to one of abandonment by his father, the move to a welfare hotel and, at the beginning of the story, the disappearance of his mother who, with the added burden of a difficult pregnancy, is unable to cope with the daily struggle for survival. Clay eventually comes to a small park scornfully called Monkey Island for the homeless who live there. Here he is taken in by two men who share the wooden crate that offers them some shelter from the cold November winds. These three become a sort of family, holding on to some sense of humanity in a brutal and brutalizing world. For all of its harshness, *Monkey Island* is also a romanticized view of the world. Although Clay is not spared the hunger, fear, illness, and squalor of the streets, there is still a distancing from the more immediate types of violence that exist there. He is always on the edge of such danger, but no incidents actually touch him. In the end, it is pneumonia that brings him back into the social services system. After ten days in the hospital, the boy is placed in a foster home and shortly thereafter is reunited with his mother and baby sister in a conclusion that readers desire but that may strain credibility. This is a carefully crafted, thoughtful book, and one in which the flow of language both sustains a mood of apprehension and encourages readers to consider carefully the plight of the homeless, recognizing unique human beings among the nameless, faceless masses most of us have learned not to see.

The Moonlight Man
1986

Grades 6–10—Fox has always been adept at writing apparently simple stories which on closer examination prove to explore the essential meaning of relationships through carefully chosen incident and to illuminate our understanding of the human condition through the vicissitudes of her characters. In this case, fifteen-year-old Catherine Ames vacations in a cottage in Nova Scotia with a father whom she barely knows—a failed writer with a poet's philosophical tongue who is an alcoholic. A competent child/woman, Catherine, in a few days of trying to understand and cope, lives through the classic kaleidoscope of responses of family members to alcoholics: denial, anger, fear, loneliness, exhaustion, disgust, pity, grief, sympathy. Harry Ames binges, blames, makes unreasonable demands, apologizes, reforms, relapses. Catherine succeeds in admiring her father for his talents while deploring his behavior, strengthened by knowing that their time together will end soon. And end it does, in apparent friendship, yet Harry Ames' last words to his daughter suggest that he will not see her again. There's enough detail and incident about alcoholism here for a case study, but the story rises above the clinical in poignantly dramatizing the separation that differing life patterns can inflict on those who love one another.

Western Wind
1993

Grades 5–8—Elizabeth Benedict, eleven, has always enjoyed the company of her eccentric artist grandmother, but when her parents insist that she spend a month with her at her rustic summer cottage off the coast of Maine, the girl feels as though she's being exiled so her parents can spend more time with her new baby brother. Anger and jealousy gnaw at her, until, almost in spite of herself, she begins to experience and appreciate the quiet beauty of Pring Island. The rather abrasive elder Benedict at times embarrasses her grand-daughter, quoting poetry and posing probing questions, while at the same time, revealing stories about her youth, her husband, and herself. At once charmed and exasperated by the island's only other inhabitants' over-zealous, impulsive young son, Elizabeth spends time with him and learns to accept the wisdom he innocently reveals. His disappearance exposes some other truths, including the real reason she's been sent to spend time with Gran. In this wonderfully realized, sensational novel, Fox's unadorned prose is anything but austere. In a forthright manner, she sets each scene and paints her thoroughly compelling, complex characters. Readers may not like them all, but they will definitely be interested in them.

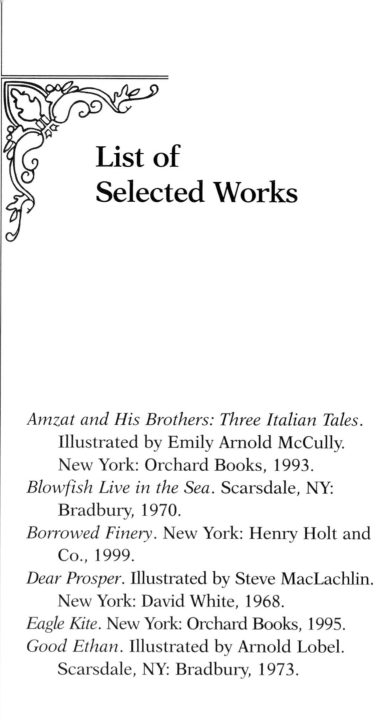

List of
Selected Works

Amzat and His Brothers: Three Italian Tales.
  Illustrated by Emily Arnold McCully.
  New York: Orchard Books, 1993.
Blowfish Live in the Sea. Scarsdale, NY:
  Bradbury, 1970.
Borrowed Finery. New York: Henry Holt and
  Co., 1999.
Dear Prosper. Illustrated by Steve MacLachlin.
  New York: David White, 1968.
Eagle Kite. New York: Orchard Books, 1995.
Good Ethan. Illustrated by Arnold Lobel.
  Scarsdale, NY: Bradbury, 1973.

How Many Miles to Babylon? Illustrated by
    Paul Giovanopoulos. New York: David
    White, 1967.
A Likely Place. Illustrated by Edward Ardizzone.
    New York: Macmillan, 1967.
Lily and the Lost Boy. New York: Orchard
    Books, 1987.
The Little Swineherd and Other Tales. Illustrated
    by Robert Byrd. New York: Dutton
    Children's Books, 1996.
Maurice's Room. Illustrated by Ingrid Fetz. New
    York: Macmillan, 1966.
Monkey Island. New York: Orchard Books, 1991.
The Moonlight Man. Scarsdale, NY:
    Bradbury, 1986.
One-Eyed Cat. Scarsdale, NY: Bradbury, 1984.
A Place Apart. New York: Farrar,
    Strauss, 1980.
Portrait of Ivan. Illustrated by Saul Lambert.
    Scarsdale, NY: Bradbury, 1969.
Radiance Descending. New York: DK, 1997.
The Slave Dancer. Illustrated by Eros
    Keith. Santa Barbara, CA: ABC-CLIO,
    1988.
The Stone-Faced Boy. Illustrated by
    Donald A. Mackay. Scarsdale, NY:
    Bradbury, 1968.

The Village by the Sea. New York: Orchard
    Books, 1988.
Western Wind. New York: Orchard Books, 1993.

List of Selected Awards

Guggenheim Fellowship (1972)
National Endowment for the Arts
    Grant (1974)
National Institute of Arts and Letters
    Award (1972)
Rockefeller Foundation Grant (1984)

***Blowfish Live in the Sea* (1970)**
National Books Award children's book
    category finalist (1971)

***The Little Swineherd and Other
Tales* (1978)**
National Book Award nomination (1979)

The Moonlight Man **(1986)**
New York Times Notable Book (1986)

A Place Apart **(1980)**
American Book Award (1983)
New York Times Outstanding Book (1980)

One-Eyed Cat **(1984)**
Newbery Honor Book (1985)
New York Times Notable Book (1984)

The Slave Dancer **(1973)**
Newbery Medal, American Library
    Association (1974)

The Village by the Sea **(1988)**
Newbery Honor Book (1989)

Glossary

absolution Forgiveness.

alienation Emotional isolation, feeling alone or like an outsider.

amputation A removal by or as if by cutting, especially the surgical removal of a limb or digit.

anaconda A very large snake found in South America.

apprehension Anxiety, concern, or worry.

armistice A truce.

austere Severe or stern.

authenticity Believability or truth.

authority A forceful or convincing voice.

autobiography One's story of one's own life; memoir.

avid Enthusiastic.

bestial Resembling a beast in character or appearance.

captivity Any place where one cannot leave or move around freely.

captor One that has captured a person or animal.

cascade A waterfall or series of small waterfalls.

cauldron A large kettle or vat used for boiling.

chaos Confusion and disorder.

characterization The act of developing a character.

compassion Understanding other people's circumstances or putting oneself in their shoes.

confidant A person to whom one might tell secrets.

consent Permission.

custody The responsibility for another person, especially a child.

depicted Portrayed.

dictator An absolute and often oppressive ruler.

Dostoevsky, Fyodor Famous Russian novelist who lived from 1821 to 1881 and who wrote *Notes from the Underground* (1864), *Crime and Punishment* (1866), and *The Brothers Karamazov* (1879–80).

Down's syndrome A genetic condition that causes mild to severe retardation.

eccentric Strange and quirky.

eloquent Extremely well-spoken or vividly expressed.

embody To represent an idea in human form.

erratic Unpredictable and changeable.

estranged Separated emotionally for a long time.

exploited Used unfairly.

facet A feature or element of something.

fictional Imaginary or make-believe.

fife A small flute with six to eight finger holes and no keys.

gimmicky Using a new scheme or angle.

grunge Rock music incorporating elements of punk rock and heavy metal, popular in the late 1980s and early 1990s.

Guggenheim Fellowship Important award given annually to writers and artists.

Hans Christian Andersen Award Award presented every other year for lifetime achievement to children's authors and illustrators.

impeding Opposing or obstructing.

judgmental Critical or lacking understanding.

kidskin A soft leather made from the skin of a young goat.

manipulate To control someone's actions or feelings by unfair or dishonest means.

melancholy Sadness or depression.

memoir A story of one's life told from personal experience, or a biography.

metaphor In writing, when one thing is used to symbolize or represent something else.

mock To make fun of.

narrative The telling of an event through a story.

narrative tension The suspense that drives a story forward and keeps the reader engaged.

organic Natural, or made from living materials.

palpable Visible.

pick-up sticks An old-fashioned game for kids involving sticks one must gather within a certain amount of time.

pygmies Any of a small people of equatorial Africa ranging under five feet in height.

quivering Shaking.

rampant Widespread.

satirize To mock or ridicule.

scandalous Shocking or outrageous.

sentimentality Emotion for the sake of

emotion; based on feeling rather than thought.

social welfare agency Government organization that provides homes for kids who have been neglected by their parents.

suitor A man who is romantically interested in a woman.

tenacity Stubborn bravery or persistence.

themes The ideas in a novel or story that reappear in different forms.

tone In a story, the mood or feeling created by the words.

vicissitudes Sudden or unexpected changes that often occur in one's life.

vulnerable Capable of being hurt.

Wilder, Thornton American playwright and novelist whose works reflect human nature and universal truths.

For More Information

Due to the changing nature of Internet links, the Rosen Publishing Group, Inc., has developed an online list of Web sites related to the subject of this book. This site is updated regularly. Please use this link to access the list:

http://www.rosenlinks.com/lab/pfox

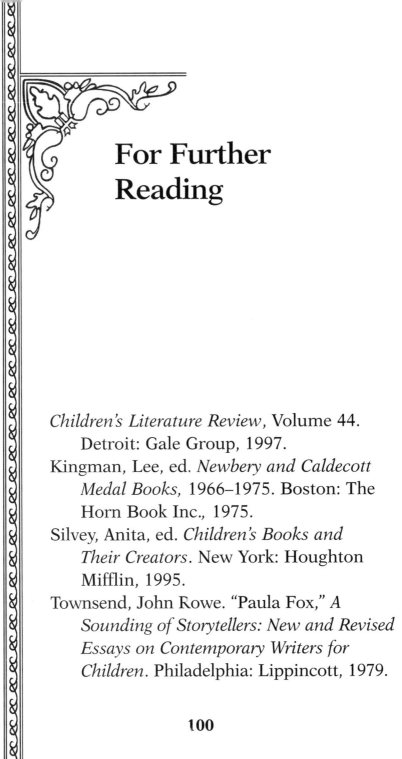

For Further Reading

Children's Literature Review, Volume 44. Detroit: Gale Group, 1997.

Kingman, Lee, ed. *Newbery and Caldecott Medal Books,* 1966–1975. Boston: The Horn Book Inc., 1975.

Silvey, Anita, ed. *Children's Books and Their Creators*. New York: Houghton Mifflin, 1995.

Townsend, John Rowe. "Paula Fox," *A Sounding of Storytellers: New and Revised Essays on Contemporary Writers for Children*. Philadelphia: Lippincott, 1979.

Bibliography

Broderick, Dorothy M. *New York Times Book Review*, November 9, 1969, (Part 2), p. 34.

Children's Literature Review, Vol. 16, 1989, Vol. 16, pp. 80, 255–269.

Fox, Paula. "About This Author." Random House. 2002. Retrieved January 2003 (http://www.randomhouse.com/teachers/authors/pfox.html).

Fox, Paula. *Borrowed Finery*. New York: Henry Holt and Co., 2001.

Fox, Paula. "Some Thoughts on Imagination in Children's Literature,"

Celebrating Children's Books: Essays on Children's Literature in Honor of Zena Sutherland. Betsy Hearne and Marilyn Kaye, eds. New York: Lothrop, Lee, and Shepard Books, 1981.

Fox, Paula. *Monkey Island*. New York: Orchard Books, 1991.

Fox, Paula. *The Slave Dancer*. Santa Barbara, CA: ABC-CLIO, 1988.

Hanscom, Leslie. "A Talk with Paula Fox: Consulting the Child Within," *Newsday*, December 13, 1987, p. 18.

Hawthorne, Mary. "Advancing Through Water," *New Yorker*, July 2, 2001.

Hedblad, Alan, ed. *Something About the Author*, Vol. 120. Detroit: Gale Group, 2000.

Literature Resource Center. Gale Group, 2002. Retrieved November, 2002 (http://www.galenet.com).

McGee, Celia. "Author Pages Through a Painful Past," *New York Daily News*, October 4, 2001, p. 55.

Sutherland, Zena. *Bulletin of the Center for Children's Books*. Chicago: University of Chicago, February 1970.

Townsend, John Rowe. *A Surrounding of Storytellers: New and Revised Essays on*

Contemporary Writers for Children. Philadelphia: Lippincott, 1979.

Tyler, Anne. "Staking Out Her Territory," *New York Times Book Review,* November 9, 1980, p. 55.

Source Notes

Chapter 1

1. Paula Fox, *Borrowed Finery* (New York: Henry Holt and Co., 2001), p. 64.
2. Paula Fox, *Celebrating Children's Books: Essays on Children's Literature in Honor of Zena Sutherland*. Betsy Hearne and Marilyn Kaye, eds. (New York: Lothrop, Lee, and Shepard Books, 1981), pp. 24–34.
3. Fox, *Borrowed Finery*, p. 74.
4. Ibid., p. 132.
5. Paula Fox. "About This Author," Random House, 2002. Retrieved March 2003 (http://www.randomhouse.com/teachers/authors/pfox.html).
6. Fox, *Borrowed Finery*, p. 127.
7. Ibid., p. 129.

Chapter 2

1. Paula Fox, *Borrowed Finery* (New York: Henry Holt and Co., 2001), p. 139.
2. Ibid., p. 149.
3. Ibid., p. 183.

Chapter 3

1. *Literature Resource Center*, Gale Group, 2002. Retrieved March 2003 (http://www.galenet.com).
2. Paula Fox, *Borrowed Finery* (New York: Henry Holt and Co., 2001), p. 18.
3. Fox, *Borrowed Finery*, p. 209.
4. Ibid.
5. Ibid., p. 210.
6. Mary Hawthorne, "Advancing Through Water," *New Yorker,* July 2, 2001.
7. Celia McGee, "Author Pages Through a Painful Past," *New York Daily New*s, October 4, 2001, p. 55.
8. Hawthorne.

Chapter 4

1. Zena Sutherland, *Bulletin of the Center for Children's Books* (Chicago: University of Chicago, February 1970), p. 96.
2. Dorothy M. Broderick, *New York Times Book Review*, November 9, 1969, Part 2, p. 34.
3. *Literature Resource Center*, Gale Group, 2002. Retrieved March 2003 (http://www.galenet.com).

4. John Rowe Townsend, *A Surrounding of Storytellers: New and Revised Essays on Contemporary Writers for Children* (New York: J. B. Lippincott, 1979), pp. 55–65.

5. Ibid.

6. Alan Hedblad, ed., *Something About the Author*, Vol. 120 (Detroit: Gale Group, 2000), pp. 106.

7. *Children's Literature Review*, Vol. 16 (Detroit: Gale Group), pp. 80, 255–269.

8. Paula Fox, *The Slave Dancer* (New York: Laurel Leaf, 1974), p. 1.

9. Paula Fox, *One-Eyed Cat* (Scarsdale, NY: Bradbury, 1984), pp. 1–2.

10. Paula Fox, *Monkey Island* (New York: Orchard Books, 1991), pp. 1–2.

11. *Literature Resource Center*, Gale Group, 2002. Retrieved March 2003 (http://www.galenet.com).

12. Anne Tyler, "Staking Out Her Territory," *New York Times Book Review*, November 9, 1980, p. 55.

13. *Children's Literature Review*, Vol. 16, 1982, Detroit: Gale Group, pp. 80, 255–269.

Chapter 5

1. Paula Fox, "About This Author." Random House, 2002. Retrieved February 2003 (http://www.randomhouse.com/teachers/authors/pfox.html).

2. Paula Fox, *Celebrating Children's Books: Essays on Children's Literature in Honor of Zena Sutherland*, Betsy Hearne and Marilyn Kaye, eds. (New York: Lothrop, Lee, and Shepard Books, 1981), pp. 24–34.

Index

About the Author:

Susanna Daniel is a fiction writer from South Florida who teaches creative writing at the University of Wisconsin at Madison. She has a BA from Columbia University and an MFA from the University of Iowa writers' workshop. Her fiction has been published in Harcourt's *Best New American Voices 2001*, *Epoch*, and *The Madison Review*, and she is currently at work on a novel.

Photo Credits

Cover and p. 2 © AP Photo/Gino Domenico

Designer: Tahara Hasan; Editor: Annie Sommers